TU PARLES!

COMMUNICATIVE ACTIVITIES IN FRENCH

by

Vee Harris and Liz Roselman

Book A

Nelson

Thomas Nelson and Sons Ltd
Nelson House   Mayfield Road
Walton-on-Thames   Surrey
KT12 5PL   UK

51 York Place
Edinburgh
EH1 3JD   UK

Thomas Nelson (Hong Kong) Ltd
Toppan Building 10/F
22A Westlands Road
Quarry Bay   Hong Kong

Thomas Nelson Australia
102 Dodds Street
South Melbourne   Victoria 3205
Australia

Nelson Canada
1120 Birchmount Road
Scarborough   Ontario
M1K 5G4   Canada

Acknowledgements
Illustrations: Jake Tebbit
Cover: David Lock

First published by E J Arnold and Son Ltd 1986
ISBN 0-560-00804-X

This edition published by Thomas Nelson and Sons Ltd 1990
ISBN 0-17-439444-6
NPN 9 8 7 6 5 4

Printed in Hong Kong

Contents

Introduction

Get talking

The purpose of this book is to help you to talk in French. It puts you in some of the situations you may encounter during a visit to France or if you meet French people in Britain.

Two books

There are two books, one for you and a slightly different one for your partner, because you each have a different part to play in each situation. One of you will have a piece of information or an opinion that the other person wants to find out about.

Tourist situations

The first twelve tasks are based on situations you might come across as a tourist in France:

For example . . . finding out if there is room in a campsite or finding out what time a particular train leaves.

In these situations, partner A will be asking about space in the campsite, or train times, while partner B will be giving the relevant details using the information contained in the B book.

Personal situations

The last eight tasks in the book are based on the sort of conversation you may have when people ask you about yourself, your family, your likes and dislikes or your summer holidays.

It is sometimes very difficult to talk about yourself, either because your partner already knows you quite well or quite simply because you do not know where to start. This is why you will be given a new identity or some 'imaginary' likes and dislikes for practice, first of all.

Using the books

- Before you start to tackle a task, look at the left-hand page. This gives you the words and phrases that you will need. Check that you know them well.
- The cartoon-strip at the bottom of the page gives you an example of how to tackle the first situation on the next page. Practise reading it with your partner.

  Then you will be ready to tackle the five other situations. Treat each one as a new conversation. Don't be worried about making mistakes – you will probably not get it right the first time. What matters most is to get the message across.
- At the bottom of the page there is a result grid so that you can record what you have found out from your partner. Copy the grid into your exercise book and fill it in for each conversation you have.
- If you finish the different conversations before other members of the class, turn to the back of the book where there are some extra activities for you and your partner to try.

Useful phrases

Here are some general words and phrases that may be useful in all the situations.

1. These you will need for every conversation:

To start a conversation
Bonjour, Monsieur/Madame/Mademoiselle
Salut, Pierre/Jeanne
Pardon Monsieur/Madame/Mademoiselle
Excusez-moi . . .
S'il vous plaît . . .

To end a conversation
Bon, d'accord/oui/ok
Bonne journée/bonne nuit
Bon après-midi/bonsoir
A demain/à bientôt/à jeudi . . .
Au revoir

2. These you may need if you or your partner are having difficulties getting the message across:

To indicate you have not understood
Comment?
Pardon?
Je ne comprends pas
Répète ça, s'il te plaît
Répétez ça, s'il vous plaît

To check you have understood
. . . n'est-ce pas?
. . . c'est bien ça?

To check someone understands you
Tu comprends?
Vous comprenez?

To get some help with your French
Comment dit-on . . . en français?
Ça s'écrit comment?

To give yourself time to think
Euh . . .
Eh bien . . .
C'est à dire . . .
Alors . . .
Mais . . .

3. These you may need to help the conversation sound more natural:

To thank someone
Merci
Merci bien/beaucoup

To respond to thanks
Je t'en prie
Je vous en prie

To apologise
Je suis désolé(e)

To respond to an apology
Ça ne fait rien
Tant pis

To show you are listening
Ah . . . oui/bon/bien

To show surprise or disbelief
Tiens!
Vraiment?
C'est vrai?

To show pleasure
C'est bien/super/formidable ça
Bravo!
Chouette!
Quelle chance!

To show sympathy or displeasure
Oh là là!
Mince alors!
C'est dommage
C'est affreux ça!

To show agreement
Oui, d'accord
Bien sûr
Je sais

To show disagreement
Je ne suis pas d'accord
Mais non
Si (when contradicting)

To show indifference
Bof!
Peut-être
Cela m'est égal

To stress what you are saying
Moi, je . . .

Les numéros

1	un (une)	11	onze	21	vingt et un
2	deux	12	douze	22	vingt-deux etc . . .
3	trois	13	treize	30	trente
4	quatre	14	quatorze	40	quarante
5	cinq	15	quinze	50	cinquante
6	six	16	seize	60	soixante
7	sept	17	dix-sept	70	soixante-dix
8	huit	18	dix-huit	80	quatre-vingts
9	neuf	19	dix-neuf	90	quatre-vingt-dix
10	dix	20	vingt	100	cent

On fait du camping

Préparation

Vous avez un emplacement pour..................?

une petite tente/une grande tente/deux petites tentes/une caravane

Il y a l'emplacement numéro x
Non, je suis désolé(e)

C'est..   complet

combien?

C'est pour ....   combien de personnes?

x personnes

C'est..   x francs par nuit

bien

trop cher

C'est pour ....   combien de nuits?

x nuit(s)/semaine(s)

You are a tourist who has just arrived at a campsite in France. Your partner is the campsite manager. You want to find out if there is any space left on the site and whether you can afford it.

The pictures show you:

(a) the size of space you need and for how many people

(b) how long you want to stay

(c) the most you can afford to pay.

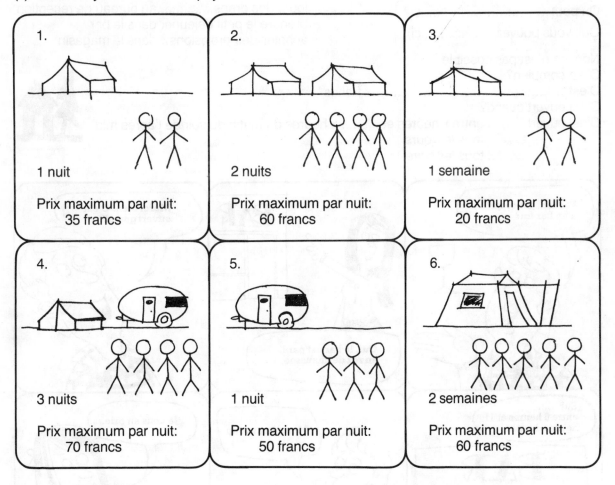

1.

1 nuit

Prix maximum par nuit:
35 francs

2.

2 nuits

Prix maximum par nuit:
60 francs

3.

1 semaine

Prix maximum par nuit:
20 francs

4.

3 nuits

Prix maximum par nuit:
70 francs

5.

1 nuit

Prix maximum par nuit:
50 francs

6.

2 semaines

Prix maximum par nuit:
60 francs

Copy out the grid below. If you manage to get a space in the campsite, write the number of the space in the appropriate box. If there is no space available or if you cannot afford it, put a cross.

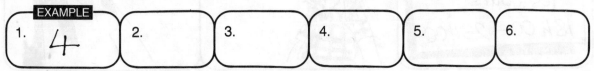

EXAMPLE

1. 4   2.   3.   4.   5.   6.

On va à l'auberge de jeunesse

Préparation

Est-ce qu'il y a.......................................ici?

Oui, c'est.............................. ⎤

La cuisine est........................... ⎥

Le bar est .... ⎦

Non, il n'y en a pas

On peut ....ici? ⎤

Oui, vous pouvez................(ici). ⎦

Non, ce n'est pas possible

C'est combien?

C'est ....x francs

C'est ouvert quand?

C'est ouvert .... entre x heures et .... x heures du matin/du soir/de l'après-midi

.... tous les jours

.... tous les soirs

un bar/une salle de jeux/une cuisine
au rez-de-chaussée
au premier étage
au deuxième étage
par là

louer des draps...............au bureau de réception
prendre le petit déjeuner dans le bar
acheter des provisions...dans le magasin

You are a tourist who has just arrived at a French youth hostel. Your partner is the warden. You want to find out about the facilities at the hostel. The pictures show you what you specifically want to ask about.

1. Où? Quand?

2. Où? Quand?

3. Thé — Où? Quand?

4. Où? Quand?

5. Où? Combien?

6. Où? Combien?

Copy out the grid below. If the hostel has the facilities you want, write down the information you are given in the appropriate box. If the facility is not available, put a cross.

1 EXAMPLE	2.	3.
Bar on ground floor. Open from 6.00 pm until 11.00pm		

4.	5.	6.

On achète des cadeaux

Préparation

Je cherche un cadeau pour mon ....   oncle/grand-père/copain
                       ma ....   mère/voisine/sœur

Qu'est-ce qu'il aime?
Qu'est-ce qu'elle aime?
Il/elle aime ....   les porte-feuilles/les bibelots/les bijoux/
                                             les porte-clés

Il/elle collectionne ....   les cartes postales/les poupées
Il/elle a besoin d' ....   une cravate/un mouchoir/un briquet/
                                             un stylo

Nous avons des ....à x francs/centimes   boîtes de chocolats/colliers/
                                             flacons de parfum

C'est trop ....   cher/grand
Je vais prendre ....   ça
                                             le parfum/la cravate

Je vous fais un paquet

You are a tourist shopping for presents in a French souvenir shop. Your partner is the sales assistant. The written information tells you:

(a) who the present is for

(b) what kind of things they like or need

(c) how much you can afford.

1. **mère**	**2.** **copain**	**3.** **voisine**
aime: le parfum les chocolats Prix maximum: 50 francs	aime: la musique collectionne: les porte-clés Prix maximum: 20 francs	aime: les bijoux collectionne: les poupées Prix maximum: 15 francs
4. **oncle**	**5.** **sœur**	**6.** **grand-père**
aime: les bonbons a besoin d'un porte-feuille Prix maximum: 20 francs	collectionne: les bibelots a besoin d'un stylo Prix maximum: 30 francs	collectionne: les cartes postales a besoin d'une cravate Prix maximum: 20 francs

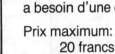

Copy out the grid below. If you make a purchase, write what you bought and how much it cost in the appropriate box.

1. EXAMPLE	2.	3.
cadeau *chocolates* prix *25 francs*	cadeau .... prix	cadeau .... prix ....
4.	5.	6.
cadeau .... prix	cadeau .... prix	cadeau .... prix ....

On fait les courses

Préparation

Vous désirez?
Je voudrais ....
Vous avez ....?

un poulet rôti
un Camembert
un kilo de . . . sucre/poires
cinq cents grammes de . . . carottes/
champignons/bananes/fraises/saucisson
deux cent cinquante grammes de . . . pâté/gruyère
un paquet de . . . chips/thé/beurre
un pot de . . . confiture/yaourt
un litre de . . . lait/vin rouge
une boîte de . . . sardines/petits pois
une bouteille de . . . limonade/jus d'orange
d' . . . eau minérale

Voilà
Ça fait combien?
Ça fait x francs
Et avec ça?
Alors, c'est tout?
Je suis désolé(e)
Il n'y en a plus
Voici x francs
Et voici votre monnaie

Bonjour. Vous désirez?

Je voudrais 500 grammes de bananes.

Voilà les bananes.

Ça fait combien?

Ça fait 5 francs. Et avec ça?

Je voudrais deux litres de lait, s'il vous plaît.

Je suis désolée, il n'y en a plus.

Bon – alors, un paquet de beurre.

Voilà, c'est tout?

Oui, ça fait combien?

Ça fait 12 francs.

Voici 20 francs.

Merci, et voici votre monnaie.

You are on a camping holiday in France and you have been asked to do the shopping. Your partner works in a grocer's shop. Your shopping list tells you what you need to buy.

1.
500 grammes
de bananes
2 litres de lait
1 paquet de
beurre

2.
250 grammes de
pâté
1 boîte de
sardines
1 bouteille d'eau
minérale
500 grammes de
fraises

3.
2 pots de yaourt
1 paquet de chips
1 Camembert
2 bouteilles de
limonade

4.
1 litre de vin
rouge
500 grammes
de carottes
1 paquet de thé
1 poulet rôti

5.
500 grammes
de champignons
1 kilo de poires
1 kilo de carottes
un poulet rôti
un kilo de
sucre

6.
1 pot de
confiture
un bouteille de
jus d'orange
2 pots de yaourt
250 grammes de
gruyère
500 grammes de
saucisson

Copy out the grid below. In the appropriate box write down the total cost of what you bought. Put a tick if you were able to buy everything on your list. If you couldn't get everything, write down what you still need to buy.

1. EXAMPLE	2.	3.
Prix total:	Prix total:	Prix total:
12 F Need milk	....	....

4.	5.	6.
Prix total:	Prix total:	Prix total:
....	....	....

5

On prend le train

Préparation

A quelle heure est-ce que le prochain train part pour .... + *place name*?
Il part à ....x heures ⎫ .... ⎫ et quart/et demie
Le prochain train part à......................midi ⎰ .... ⎰ moins le quart
A quelle heure est-ce que le train arrive à .... + *place name*?
Il arrive à .... + *time*
Il part de quel quai?
Quai numéro........................... + *number*
C'est combien?
Aller simple ou aller-retour?
Ça fait...francs
Voilà

<table>
<tr><td colspan="2" align="center">24 HOUR CLOCK</td></tr>
</table>

24 HOUR CLOCK
Most timetables use the 24 hour clock.
Here is a table of equivalent times.

1.00 pm = 13 heures (treize heures)
2.00 pm = 14 heures (quatorze heures)
3.00 pm = 15 heures (quinze heures)
4.00 pm = 16 heures (seize heures)
5.00 pm = 17 heures (dix-sept heures)
6.00 pm = 18 heures (dix-huit heures)
7.00 pm = 19 heures (dix-neuf heures)
8.00 pm = 20 heures (vingt heures)
9.00 pm = 21 heures (vingt et une heures)
10.00 pm = 22 heures (vingt-deux heures)
11.00 pm = 23 heures (vingt-trois heures)
12.00 pm = 24 heures (vingt-quatre heures)

You are a tourist travelling in France and your partner works in the ticket office at a railway station in Paris. The written information tells you which town you are going to. You need to find out:

(a) what time your train leaves

(b) what time it will arrive

(c) which platform it leaves from

(d) how much your ticket will cost.

Copy out the grid and write down the information as you receive it.

EXAMPLE

1.
DESTINATION
CALAIS
Départ ....9:00 a.m.......
Arrivée ...12:00 p.m.......
Quai ....1..............
Prix

200 Francs

2.
DESTINATION
LILLE
Départ ....
Arrivée ....
Quai ....
Prix

3.
DESTINATION
DIEPPE
Départ ....
Arrivée ....
Quai ....
Prix

4.
DESTINATION
ROUEN
Départ ....
Arrivée ....
Quai ....
Prix

5.
DESTINATION
BOULOGNE
Départ ....
Arrivée ....
Quai ....
Prix

6.
DESTINATION
AMIENS
Départ ....
Arrivée ....
Quai ....
Prix

On va au syndicat d'initiative

Préparation

Vous avez.................?	un plan de............................
	un dépliant sur ....
	une liste des hôtels de ....
	une liste des campings de ...
	une carte de la région..........

+ name of town or region

Oui, voilà
C'est combien?
C'est........................   x francs/gratuit
Voilà, les ....   x francs
Non, je suis désolé(e), il n'y en a plus
Tant pis
Qu'est-ce qu'il y a à voir à ....?   *+ name of town*
Il y a.........................   le port/le marché/le casino/le musée/le château/
le monument/le phare/la plage/la vieille ville/la cathédrale/l'église
Et puis il y a...............   les magasins aussi
Formidable, merci bien

16

You are a tourist visiting the north of France. You want to find out about some of the towns in the area. Your partner works in a tourist information office. The written information tells you the things you want to ask for. You should check whether you have to pay for the maps.

Ask your partner what there is to see in the town.

1. **BOULOGNE**	2. **CALAIS**	3. **DIEPPE**
plan de la ville (prix?)	dépliant	liste des hôtels
dépliant	les choses à voir	plan de la ville (prix?)
les choses à voir	carte de la région (prix?)	les choses à voir

4. **ROUEN**	5. **FÉCAMP**	6. **DEAUVILLE**
plan de la ville (prix?)	liste des campings	liste des hôtels
dépliant	carte de la région (prix?)	plan de la ville (prix?)
les choses à voir	les choses à voir	les choses à voir

Copy out the grid below. In the appropriate box, write down what your partner gives you and any places in the town (s)he recommends you to visit.

EXAMPLE **BOULOGNE**	**CALAIS**	**DIEPPE**
Map - 7 francs + brochure — see old town, port and shops.		

ROUEN	**FÉCAMP**	**DEAUVILLE**

On demande son chemin

Préparation

Pour aller .... à .... la banque/la poste/la cathédrale, s'il vous plaît?
.... au .... musée/château/marché, s'il vous plaît?
Oui, c'est dans................. la rue................. *+ name*
sur ....le boulevard/le cours................. *+ name*
Vous allez tout droit
Vous allez jusqu'à la place de la Victoire
Vous prenez................ la première/deuxième rue................ à droite
.... à gauche

Vous traversez la place
Puis vous tournez............... } à gauche
Et c'est........................... } à droite

C'est dans quelle rue?
Oui, c'est ça

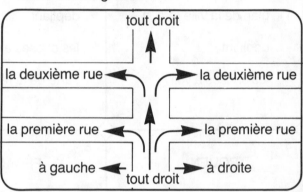

C'est dans quelle rue?
Oui, c'est ça

You are a tourist who has just arrived at the railway station in a French town. There are several places you want to go in the town – the pictures show you the places you want to go to. You ask your partner, who lives in the town, for directions to each place. The boxes on the map mark the main buildings and tourist attractions.

Listen carefully to the directions you are given, and in the grid write down the correct letter of each place and its street name.

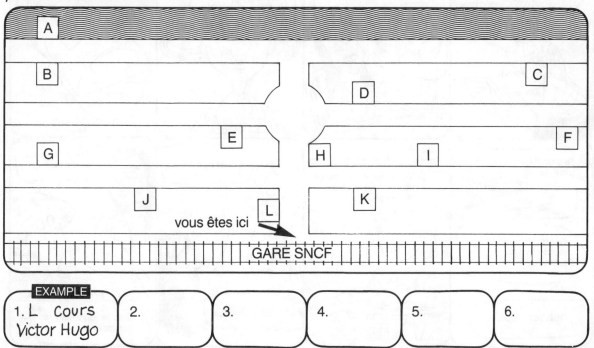

On va au café

Préparation

Vous désirez?
Je voudrais........................ un café/une bière etc. ⎫
                                  un sandwich/une glace ⎭ s'il vous plaît
Qu'est-ce que vous voulez comme sandwich?
Un sandwich.................... au pâté/au fromage/au jambon/au saucisson
Une glace simple ou double?
A quel(s) parfum(s)?
Une glace........................ au chocolat/au café/à la vanille/à la fraise
Très bien
Tout de suite
Je suis désolé(e), il n'y a plus de......................... + *item*
Alors, vous avez ....? + *alternative item*
Voilà ....
C'est combien?
Ça fait .... francs
Le service est compris?
Oui, le service est compris/Non, le service n'est pas compris

You are a customer in a cafe in France. The menu shows you what is normally available at the cafe. The pictures beneath it show you what you want to order and the most you can afford. It is up to you what kind of hot or cold drink you want. If you cannot afford exactly what you want, choose something different.

Café de la Gare — Bar-brasserie
Rue du Bac

Menu

Boissons	prix
café	5,00F
café-crème	10,00F
chocolat chaud	9,50F
thé	12,00F
limonade	4,50F
coca	6,00F
diabolo-menthe	7,50F
grenadine	8,00F
panaché	10,00F
bière	10,00F

Casse-croûtes	prix
croque-monsieur	15,00F
pizza	13,00F
sandwichs:	10,00F
pâté	
fromage	
saucisson	
jambon	

Glaces

vanille
fraise
café
chocolat

simple 5,00F

double 10,00F

LA MAISON N'ACCEPTE PAS LES CHEQUES

SERVICE COMPRIS 12%

1. Prix maximum: 20F
2. Prix maximum: 20F
3. Prix maximum: 22F
4. Prix maximum: 10F
5. Prix maximum: 25F
6. Prix maximum: 16F

Copy out the grid below. In the appropriate box, write down the cost of your order.

EXAMPLE 1. 20 francs	2.	3.	4.	5.	6.

On explique un plat

Préparation

Qu'est-ce que c'est ....? le cassoulet/le couscous/
un croque-monsieur/la quiche lorraine/
la fondue/la ratatouille

C'est une sorte de...............ragoût
sauce   qu'on mange avec.........du pain
sandwich grillé   ....de la semoule
tarte

Qu'est-ce qu'il y a dedans?
Est-ce qu'il y a ....dedans? du jambon/du lard/du saucisson/
Il y a ....dedans du vin/du lait/du poulet/du fromage/
du beurre/de l'ail/des œufs/des épices/
des haricots blancs/des oignons/
des poivrons/des tomates/des aubergines/
des courgettes/des pois chiches

C'est délicieux
Vous voulez l'essayer?
Oui, je veux bien
Non, merci, je ne veux pas

Oui, je veux bien.

Qu'est-ce que c'est un croque-monsieur?

Eh bien... c'est une sorte de sandwich grillé.

Et qu'est-ce qu'il y a dedans?

Il y a du jambon et du fromage.

Ah, bon.

Vous voulez l'essayer?

Non merci, je ne veux pas.

You are a tourist in a restaurant in France. Your partner is the waiter. You don't know what some items on the menu are, so you ask the waiter about them. The names underlined on the menu tell you which items you want to find out about.

Hostellerie de la Rivière
Sorges (face à l'église) ☎ (53) 08.22.31

— *Menu* —

Nos Casse-croûtes		
1 Croque-monsieur	10,00F	
Croque-madame	12,00F	
2 Quiche lorraine	12,00F	

Hors d'œuvre		
Œuf mayonnaise	10,50F	
Demi-douzaine d'escargots	15,00F	
3 Ratatouille	12,00F	

Entrées	
4 Cassoulet	25,00F
Steak-frites	18,00F
5 Couscous au poulet	20,00F
6 Fondue savoyarde	27,00F

Desserts	
Tarte aux pommes	8,00F
Crème caramel	9,00F
Glaces	6,00F

Copy out the table below. Next to each dish, write down the main ingredients. When you have finished, decide whether or not you want to try it and tell the waiter.

Dish	Main ingredients
Croque-monsieur	bread, ham, cheese
Quiche lorraine	
Ratatouille	
Cassoulet	
Couscous	
Fondue	

EXAMPLE

On va à la pharmacie

Préparation

Je me sens malade
Qu'est-ce que vous avez?
J'ai mal .... ⎤ à la tête/à la gorge
Vous avez mal ....? ⎦ à l'estomac/à l'oreille

J'ai .... ⎤ envie de vomir
Vous avez ....? ⎱ la diarrhée
⎰ la peau brûlée

Je suis .... ⎤ enrhumé(e)
Vous êtes ....? ⎦ fatigué(e)

Vous avez de la fièvre?*   * A normal temperature is
J'ai ....x° ....de fièvre   36.4°
Je crois que vous avez .... ⎤ la grippe
⎱ une crise de foie/une infection de
⎰ l'oreille/un coup de soleil

Qu'est-ce qu'il faut faire?
Prenez ....   2 aspirines
                             3 de ces comprimés ⎤
Mettez ....   1 de ces gouttes dans l'oreille ⎱ x fois par jour
                             cette lotion ⎰

C'est tout ce qu'il faut faire?
Buvez ....   beaucoup d'eau
Ne mangez pas .....   pendant 2 jours
Ça fait combien?
Ça fait x francs

You are a tourist on holiday in France. You are not feeling very well. Your partner works in a chemist's shop. You want to find out what is wrong with you and get the treatment you need. The pictures show you your symptoms and your temperature.

Copy out the table below. Write down what the chemist tells you to do and the price of any medicine you buy.

	Treatment	Price of medicine
EXAMPLE	1. Take 2 asprins 3 times a day	15 francs
	2.	
	3.	
	4.	
	5.	
	6.	

On va à la poste

Préparation

Je voudrais envoyer.............. ⎫ une carte postale............. ⎫ en Angleterre*
                                   une lettre...................... en Ecosse*
                                   un colis .... en France
                                                                    en Irlande
                                                                    aux Etats-Unis
                                                                    au Pays de Galles*

C'est combien?
C'est ....x .... francs
Attendez, je vais ⎰ le peser *(for a parcel)*
                   ⎱ la peser *(for a letter)*

> *On published price lists these may come under the general heading of GRANDE-BRETAGNE or ROYAUME-UNI

Ça pèse ....x .... grammes/kilos
Alors, ça fait ....x...............francs
Voilà.............. ⎰ le timbre/les timbres
                   ⎱ votre monnaie

You are a tourist on holiday in France. You have various cards, letters and parcels to send to your family and friends. Your partner works in the post office. The pictures show you what you want to send and to which country.

Copy out the grid below. In the appropriate box, write the cost of the stamps you buy.

EXAMPLE
1. PRIX: 1 Franc 80

2. PRIX: ....

3. PRIX: ....

4. PRIX: ....

5. PRIX: ....

6. PRIX: ....

Préparation

J'ai perdu	mon porte-monnaie/passeport/sac/parapluie ma valise/montre
Il/elle est de quelle couleur?	
Il est	rouge/noir/vert/brun/blanc/bleu
Elle est..	rouge/noire/verte/brune/blanche/bleue
De quelle nationalité êtes-vous?	
Je suis	anglais(e)/français(e)/américain(e)
Il/elle est comment?	
(Il/elle est ....) en ....(?)	cuir/plastique/or/argent
Vous étiez où?	
Dans..	le train/car/métro/bus/taxi
Je vais regarder la liste	
On a trouvé	un/une...*object*... + *description* + *where found*
Vous avez de la chance	
C'est formidable!	
Je suis désolé(e), il n'y a pas de. . .*object*. . .sur la liste	
Zut alors! Merci quand même	

You are a tourist visiting France. You have lost something valuable and go to the police station to see if anyone has found it. The pictures show you what you have lost, and where you think you lost it.

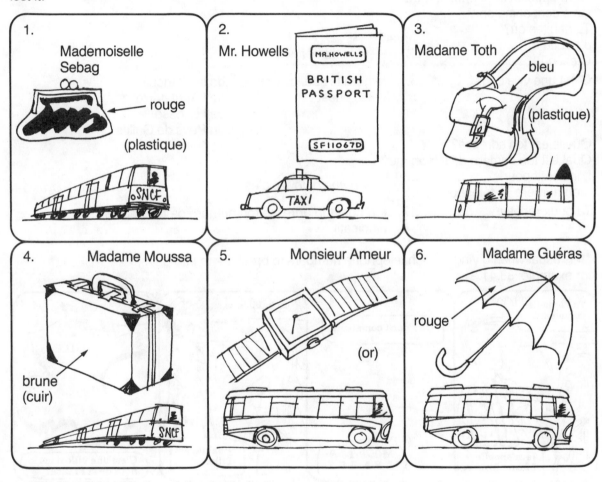

Copy out the grid below. In the appropriate box, put a tick if the lost object has been found and a cross if it has not.

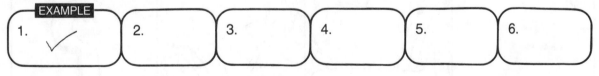

On se fait un nouvel ami

Préparation

Tu t'appelles comment?
Je m'appelle...........................
Ça s'écrit comment?
Tu habites où?
J'habite à............................. } + *name of town*
C'est où ....?

C'est une ville dans................   le nord/le sud/le centre/.....de la France
                                        l'est/l'ouest   .....de l'Angleterre
                                                                .....de l'Ecosse
                                                                .....du Pays de Galles

Quelle est ton adresse?
Quel est ton numéro de téléphone?*
L'indicatif pour..................... } + *name of town*, c'est ....
Mon numéro de téléphone à ....

Tu peux répéter ....?   ton nom/ton adresse/ton numéro de téléphone/
                                        l'indicatif

*It is usual when giving French telephone numbers to break them into pairs,
for example: 83.41.21

You are a British teenager going on holiday to France. Your partner is a young French person whom you have just met on the boat over. You want to keep in touch by writing to each other. Imagine you are the person in the written information. First, ask your partner for her/his name, address and phone number. Then give your information in answer to her/his questions.

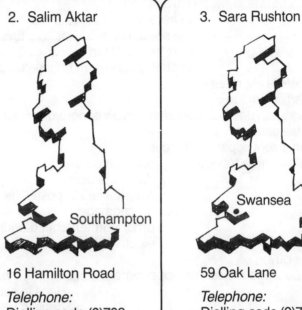

1. Tracey Sullivan

Manchester

43 Broad Street

Telephone:
Dialling code (0)61
Number 231897

2. Salim Aktar

Southampton

16 Hamilton Road

Telephone:
Dialling code (0)703
Number 823561

3. Sara Rushton

Swansea

59 Oak Lane

Telephone:
Dialling code (0)792
Number 199845

Copy out the page from the address book for each conversation you have, and fill in the information about your partner.

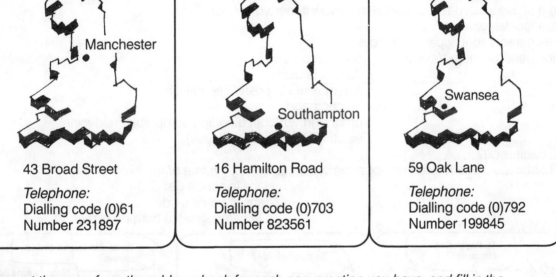

EXAMPLE

Surname... Arnoux

First Name ... Martin

Address ... 62, avenue de la Dame

Blanche, LILLE

Telephone ☎

Code ... 20

Number ... 42 · 54 ·16

On décrit sa famille

Préparation

Tu t'appelles comment?
Je m'appelle...................
Tu as ....? quel âge/des frères et des sœurs/un animal
J'ai............................. (13) ans
                           un frère, il a ....x........ ans
                           une sœur, elle a ....x........ ans
                           deux frères, Brian a ....x........ ans et Paul a ....x........ ans
                           un chat/un chien/un cobaye/un poisson rouge

Il est marié/elle est mariée
Je suis fils/fille unique
Je n'ai pas .... de .... frères/sœurs/père/mère/d'animal
Que font tes parents?
Mes parents sont séparés/divorcés
Mon père/ma mère travaille........   dans un bureau
                                       dans une usine
                                       à la mairie/à la poste/à la maison
Il/elle est ....   au chômage
                                       programmeur/chef d'équipe/comptable/médecin/
                                       électricien/coiffeur (coiffeuse)

Tu habites où?
J'habite .... une maison/un appartement .... à .... + *name of town*
                                              dans le centre de........
                                              dans la banlieue de ....
                                              à la campagne/au bord de la mer

You are a young British person on holiday in France. Your partner is a young French person you have just met. You want to find out about each other's home life. First ask your partner about her/his family. Then give your information in answer to her/his questions. Imagine you are the person in the pictures.

1. Ruth Beattie (14 ans)

Brian (20) Paul (17)
(marié)
 2 cobayes
père – programmeur
mère – au chômage

Elsfield

2. Ian Stuart (13 ans)

Julia (10) Pat (8)

père – chef d'équipe
 (usine)
mère – à la maison

Stranraer

3. Dominic Williams (15 ans)

Tony (7)

père – comptable
mère – médecin

Leicester
(centre)

Copy out the form below and for each conversation you have fill in the information about your partner.

	EXAMPLE	5	6
Nom	4. Huppert		
Prénom	Marie-Louise		
Frère(s) (prénom(s) et âge(s))			
Sœur(s) (prénom(s) et âge(s))	Claire 14 ans		
Animal	Chat		
Emploi des parents	Mère – bureau		
Domicile	Paris (banlieue)		

On cherche son correspondant ou sa correspondante

Préparation

Ecoute, tu arrives à la gare demain, mais je n'ai pas de photo de toi

Tu es comment?

Je suis .... (assez) grand(e)/petit(e)/gros(se)/mince

Comment sont tes cheveux?

J'ai les cheveux ..... blonds/noirs/marron
longs/courts/frisés/bouclés/raides

Qu'est-ce que tu vas porter?

Je vais porter .... un blouson/un manteau
un pantalon/un jean/ ....bleu/blanc/noir/vert/gris
un pull   rouge/jaune
une veste/une jupe/ ....bleue/blanche/noire/verte/grise
une robe   rouge/jaune

Tu portes des lunettes?

Je porte des lunettes (aussi)

Pas de problème maintenant

A demain

Bon voyage

Your partner is your French penfriend who is coming to stay with you. You have not seen each other before and you want to make sure you will recognise one another when you meet at the station tomorrow. You ring up to find out what your penfriend looks like. First, ask your partner to describe herself/himself. Then imagine you are the person in the pictures, and give your information in answer to your partner's questions.

Copy out the table below. For each conversation you have, draw a picture to show what your penfriend looks like and will be wearing.

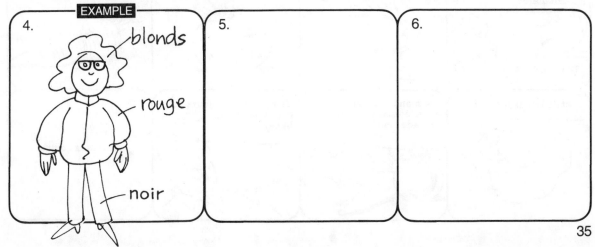

35

On parle de sa routine journalière

Préparation

Je peux vous poser des questions sur votre routine journalière?

Est-ce que vous mangez......................? ⎫   du pain complet
                                        de la salade

Je mange... ⎬   des fruits frais/des légumes frais
                                        des bonbons/des gâteaux

Est-ce que vous buvez..........................? ⎫   de l'eau
Je bois.. ⎬   du jus de fruit/du coca cola

Est-ce que vous regardez.....................? ⎫   la télévision
Je regarde .... ⎭

Est-ce que vous prenez ....? ⎫   de l'exercice
Je prends.. ⎭

Est-ce que vous vous brossez ....? ⎫   les dents
Je me brosse.. ⎭

Est-ce que vous vous couchez................? ⎫   tard
Je me couche.. ⎭

Tous les jours
Pratiquement jamais
Régulièrement
Combien .... ⎫   de fois ....   par jour/par semaine?
           .... ⎭   d'heures ....

Seulement x fois/heures par jour/par semaine
Entre 'x' et 'x' heures
Plus de 'x' heures
Avec   ⎫
            ⎬ ....chaque repas
Après   ⎭

Bonjour, je peux vous poser des questions sur votre routine journalière?

D'accord.

Tous les jours, est-ce que vous mangez...

des fruits frais?

des légumes frais?

et de la salade?

Je mange des fruits, des légumes et de la salade tous les jours.

Bien, et tous les jours, est-ce que vous buvez...?

continuez comme ça...

Sondage – Est-ce que vous négligez votre santé?

Your partner is a French person conducting a survey to find out how much daily care people take of their health. The pictures give you details about your routine. After you have answered the questions your partner will make some comments about how healthy your life style is.

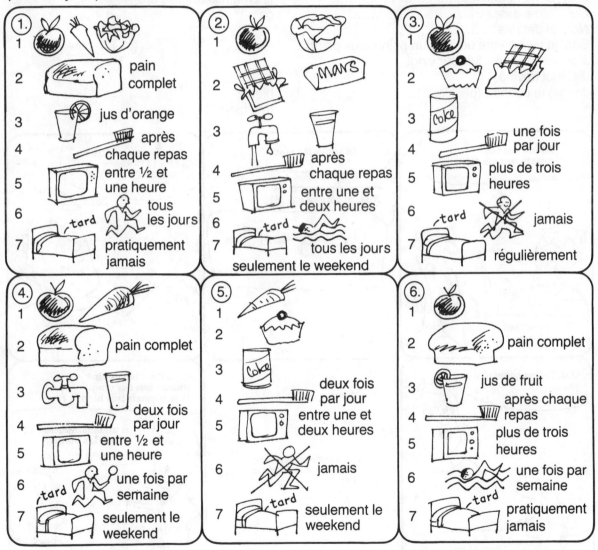

Copy out the grid below. In the appropriate box, write down the score your partner gives you.

EXAMPLE					
1.	2.	3.	4.	5.	6.

On parle de ce qu'on aime

Préparation

Alors, j'ai des questions pour toi
D'accord, vas-y
Tu aimes ....?
Oui, j'aime beaucoup ....
Oui, j'aime assez ....   les maths/l'anglais etc.
Non, je déteste ....   ça
Bon, je vais mettre un zéro/un point/deux points
J'ai bien deviné x fois sur vingt
J'ai mal deviné
Je (ne) te connais (pas) ....   bien
très bien

38

How well do you know your partner? The written information lists twenty items that they may like or dislike. Copy out the list. In the 'guesses' column, next to each item, put a score according to what you think they would say:

j'aime beaucoup = 2; j'aime assez = 1; je déteste = 0.

Then, ask your partner whether they like or dislike each item. In the 'facts' column, write down the score to show what they really do feel.

		Guesses	Facts
Les matières scolaires	1	....	....
1. les maths	2	....	....
2. l'anglais	3	....	....
3. le français	4	....	....
4. la musique	5	....	....
5. les sciences			
Les sports	6	....	....
6. le tennis	7	....	....
7. le football	8	....	....
8. le basket	9	....	....
9. la natation	10	....	....
10. le cyclisme			
Les passe-temps	11	....	....
11. aller au cinéma	12	....	....
12. aller aux discos	13	....	....
13. écouter des disques	14	....	....
14. faire la cuisine	15	....	....
15. faire du bricolage			
A la télé	16	....	....
16. les actualités	17	....	....
17. les vieux films	18	....	....
18. le sport	19	....	....
19. les feuilletons	20	....	....
20. les concours			

Count up the number of times that what you thought your partner would say and what he/she actually did say where the same. You may not know your partner as well as you thought!

On sort ensemble

Préparation

On sort ensemble......samedi?   *(+ other days of the week)*
Oui, d'accord/je veux bien
Tu es libre ....?   le matin/l'après-midi/le soir
Je suis libre ....
Je suis occupé(e)..................
Bon, tu veux.......................?   ⎫ aller........à la piscine/à la patinoire/à la disco/
                                          à la maison des jeunes/
Oui, d'accord j'aime..............   ⎬   au cinéma/au stade/au théâtre/au musée
Non, je n'aime pas................   faire les magasins
Non, je déteste....................   ⎭ jouer.......au football/au tennis
Moi, je préfère ....
Moi aussi
Bon, alors on va *+ activity* ensemble *+ day* *+ time of day*
Oui, c'est ça

You and your partner are new friends. You have rung up to arrange to go out together. The written information tells you the day and the time of day you are free and what you like and don't like doing in your free time.

1. samedi

matin	✓
après-midi	✗
soir	✓
piscine	♡ ♡
cinéma	♡
patinoire	⊗

2. dimanche

matin	✗
après-midi	✓
soir	✓
maison des jeunes	♡ ♡
disco	♡
stade	⊗

3. mardi

matin	✓
après-midi	✓
soir	✓
stade	♡ ♡
piscine	♡
disco	⊗

4. mercredi

matin	✓
après-midi	✗
soir	✓
musée	♡ ♡
patinoire	♡
tennis	⊗

5. jeudi

matin	✗
après-midi	✗
soir	✓
football	♡ ♡
disco	♡
théâtre	⊗

6. vendredi

matin	✓
après-midi	✓
soir	✗
magasins	♡ ♡
football	♡
cinéma	⊗

Copy out the page from the diary below. In the appropriate place, write down what time of day you are going out together and what you are going to do.

lundi	vendredi
	samedi *Soir- aller au cinéma* EXAMPLE
mardi	dimanche
mercredi	
jeudi	

On raconte ce qu'on a fait pendant les vacances

Préparation

Tu es allé(e) en vacances ....?	cet été/à Pâques
Oui, je suis allé(e)...................................	en France/en Espagne/en Ecosse/en Inde/ en Cornouailles
Dans quelle région?	
Dans	le nord/le sud/l'est/l'ouest
Tu as logé où?	
J'ai logé........................	chez ma tante/chez des amis/ dans une auberge de jeunesse/ dans un hôtel

à la campagne
à la montagne
au bord de la mer

Tu es resté(e) combien de temps?	
Je suis resté(e)	une semaine/deux semaines/un mois
Qu'est-ce que tu as fait?	
J'ai fait........................	des promenades ....à pied/à bicyclette de la voile/du ski nautique des excursions
J'ai joué au..................	tennis/minigolf
J'ai............................	pris des bains de soleil/nagé
Je suis	allé(e) à la pêche
Il a fait ....(?)	beau/du soleil/mauvais.........................
Il a plu........................	tous les jours

Tu es allée en vacances cet été?

Oui, je suis allée en Espagne.

Dans quelle région?

Dans l'ouest.

Tu as logé où?

Dans un hôtel au bord de la mer.

Tu es restée combien de temps?

Deux semaines.

Chouette! Qu'est-ce que tu as fait?

J'ai pris des bains de soleil...

Formidable!

et j'ai fait de la voile.

Il a fait beau?

Oui, il a fait du soleil tous les jours.

Et toi, tu es allé en vacances?

On raconte ce qu'on a fait pendant les vacances

Your partner is a friend whom you have not seen recently. You want to find out about each other's holidays. First ask your partner about her/his holiday. Then answer her/his questions about yours. The pictures show you where you went, how long you stayed and what you did.

1. Ecosse — 2 SEMAINES

2. Île de Wight — 1 SEMAINE — MINI GOLF

3. Inde — chez mes amis — 1 MOIS

Copy out the table below. For each conversation you have, fill in the details of your partner's holiday in the appropriate box.

	Vacances?	Où? Pays/région?	Logé où?	Resté(e) combien de temps?	Activités?	Temps?
4. EXAMPLE	✓	Espagne (ouest)	hôtel au bord de la mer	2 semaines	bains de soleil voile	soleil
5.						
6.						

On raconte ce qu'on a fait hier

Préparation

Vous vous appelez comment?
Je m'appelle...........................
Qu'est-ce que vous avez fait hier soir?
Vers/à ....   x heures
Je suis allé(e).........................   au casino/au restaurant/au cinéma/
                              au bar/au café/au théâtre
              ....   chez ....
J'ai quitté ....   le bureau
J'ai rendu visite à ....   ma tante à l'hôpital
Qu'est-ce que vous avez ....?   mangé/vu/fait ....au *+ place*
Qu'est-ce que vous avez fait ensuite?
J'ai gagné ....   x francs
J'ai mangé ....
J'ai rencontré mon ami ....
J'ai fait...................les courses
J'ai dîné
J'ai vu...................................
Je suis sorti(e).........................   voir un ami/une amie
Je suis rentré(e) ....   à la maison/chez moi/à pied
A quelle heure êtes-vous rentré(e) chez vous?
La voiture est tombée en panne
Je crois que vous êtes innocent(e)
Je crois que vous êtes coupable

You are a French person suspected of being one of a gang of criminals who committed a robbery at a factory last night. Your partner is a detective who wants to know your exact movements during the evening. The written information tells you what to say you did last night.

1. Monsieur Hubert

20h00 casino (gagné 1000 francs)
22h00 restaurant (poulet frites)
24h00 Bar des Amis (rencontré Luc)
01h00 rentré à la maison

2. Mademoiselle Ameur

19h30 Café de la Paix (rencontré Martin)
21h00 cinéma ('Le Témoin')
23h00 chez Martin
24h00 rentrée chez moi

3. Madame Pastaud

19h00 quitté le bureau
19h30 théâtre ('Les Mains Sales')
22h00 restaurant (gigot à l'ail)
01h00 rentrée chez moi

4. Mademoiselle de Lavenne

19h30 rendu visite à tante à l'hôpital
20h30 café (croque-monsieur)
21h00 cinéma (Superman)
23h15 rentrée chez moi

5. Monsieur Brajon

19h00 dîner à la maison (Quiche lorraine)
20h00 sorti voir un ami
22h30 voiture tombée en panne
24h00 rentré à la maison à pied

6. Madame Jacob

18h00 magasins (les courses)
19h30 dîné à la maison (steak et frites)
20h30 sortie voir une amie
22h30 rentrée chez moi.

Copy out the grid below. In the appropriate box, put a tick if the detective believed your alibi and thought you were innocent, and a cross if you said something that made the detective think you were guilty.

EXAMPLE M. Hubert ✓	Mlle Ameur	Mme Pastaud	Mlle de Lavenne	M. Brajon	Mme Jacob

TU ECRIS, TU DESSINES, TU IMAGINES

Follow-up activities

1. On fait du camping

a) Design a French poster, like the one in Book B, to advertise a campsite. You can change the details, such as how far it is from the sea, or the different facilities available. Perhaps it has a swimming pool or a bar.

b) Imagine that instead of just arriving at the campsite, you had written to reserve a space in advance. Choose one of the pictures in Book A, and fill in the blanks in this model letter with the details of what your require. Remember to sign your name at the end.

> Monsieur/Madame,
> Je vondrais réserver un emplacement pour ....(tent, caravan).... pour ...personnes.
>
> Nous arrivons le 4 Juillet et nous restons ...... nuits.
> Veuillez agréer l'expression de mes sentiments respectueux,

2. On va à l'auberge de jeunesse

Draw a plan, like the one in Book B, of your ideal, luxury youth hostel or hotel. You might want to include a hairdresser's (*coiffeur*), a sauna (*sauna*), a restaurant, or tennis courts.

3. On achète des cadeaux

Make a list of your friends and the different members of your family. Against each name, write down in French what present you might bring them back from a trip to France. Add how much, in French francs, you would expect to spend on each one.

4. On fait les courses

Write a shopping list in French of everything you would need for the perfect picnic for about five people.

5. On prend le train

For each train that you found out about, write the railway announcement that you would expect to hear as the train arrived at the station. Use this model to help you:

> Le rapide à destination de .... est annoncé au quai numéro ....

6. On va au syndicat d'initiative

Design a French poster advertising the attractions of your own town or village. Use this model to help you:

> VENEZ À ....
> VISITEZ:
>   son (musée? théâtre?
>   parc zoologique? église?)
>   sa (piscine? cathédrale?)
>   ses (restaurants? magasins?)

7. On demande son chemin

Look at the map in Book B and imagine you live next to the market. Your friends, Marc and Luc, are coming by train to see you on Friday and you write to tell them how to get to your new house from the station. Use the model letter to help you give the directions. Remember to sign your name at the end.

> Chers Marc et Luc,
> Voilà les directions pour trouver notre maison quand vous viendrez vendredi.
>
> En sortant de la gare, vous .... jusqu'à ....
> Vous ...... et notre maison est ....
> A vendredi!

Now write the letter again, but this time imagine you live next to the cathedral.

8. On va au café

Design a disgusting menu. You can imagine the worst combinations you can think of; for example *une glace au fromage'*. Draw pictures of each item and add the price in French francs.

9. On explique un plat

Write down in French how you would explain to a French person what ingredients there are in:

shandy
shepherd's pie
custard.

10. On va à la pharmacie

Draw a strip cartoon showing a Superhero inflicting blows on an enemy. Add speech bubbles to show what the enemy would say each time; for example *'Aïe, j'ai mal à la tête'*.

11. On va à la poste

Draw six letters, postcards or parcels. Address them to famous people in different parts of the world (Le Président des Etats-Unis, for example) and draw the stamp on each item showing the cost in French francs.

12. On cherche un objet perdu

a) Imagine you lost a valuable item in France but you did not have time to go to the police station before returning to Britain. Choose one of the items in Book A and write a letter to the police describing it. Use this model letter to help you. Remember to sign your name at the end.

> Monsieur/Madame,
> Pendant mes vacances en France, j'ai perdu ......
> dans .... Il / elle est ......
> et en .... Si on a trouvé ...., pourriez-vous me l'envoyer?
> Veuillez agréer l'expression de mes sentiments respectueux.

b) Draw a picture of four of your own personal belongings and label them in French to show their colour, and what they are made of.

13. On se fait un nouvel ami

Copy out the page from the French address book and fill it in with the details of your own name, address, dialling code and phone number.

14. On décrit sa famille

a) Copy out the form and fill it in with the details of you own family, pets and home.

b) Write a letter to a penpal telling her/him about yourself. Use this model letter to help you and sign your name at the end.

> Je m'appelle ....
> J'ai ....ans. J'ai ....
> (brothers and sisters). J'ai
> .... (pets).... J'habite
> .... (flat or house)...... à
> (name of town). C'est
> .... (where it is in Britain).
> Et toi, tu as quel âge ?
> Tu as des frères ou des
> sœurs ?
> Écris-moi bientôt,

15. On cherche son correspondant/sa correspondante

Draw a cartoon of a famous person. Label it in French to show the colour of their hair and eyes (*il/elle a les yeux .... et les cheveux ....*) and what they usually wear (*il/elle porte ....*).

16. On parle de sa routine journalière

Design a French poster telling people how to stay healthy. Draw pictures to illustrate the advice. Use this model to help you, and add any other of your own tips.

> TOUS LES JOURS, MANGEZ ....
> AVEC LE REPAS, BUVEZ ....
> PRENEZ DE L'EXERCICE ....
> BROSSEZ-VOUS LES DENTS ....

17. On parle de ce qu'on aime (et de ce qu'on déteste)

Make a list of your top ten likes or pet hates. (You can include anything, e.g. food, colours, animals, days of the week, seasons, etc.)

18. On sort ensemble

Draw pictures to show various people on their way somewhere and add speech bubbles to show what they are saying. For example, a couple of gangsters could be saying *'on va à la banque'*.

19. On raconte ce qu'on a fait pendant les vacances

Write a letter to your penpal, Béatrice, describing your summer holidays. You can say what you really did, or you can imagine what sort of holiday you would like to have had. Use this model letter to help you and sign your name at the end.

> Chère Béatrice,
> Tu es allée en vacances cet
> été ? Moi, je suis allé(e)
> .... (name of place). J'ai logé
> .... (hotel, youth hostel,
> friends, relatives). Je suis
> resté(e).... (length of time).
> J'ai.....et..... (activities).
> Il a fait..... (weather)....
> Je me suis bien amusé(e)
> A bientôt,

20. On raconte ce qu'on a fait hier

Imagine that there was another person involved in the crime. Make up a timetable, in French, that would show that (s)he was also guilty. For example, perhaps the person went to the doctor's for her/his cough or ate snails (*escargots*), which are usually served with garlic.